Living with Bipolar
My Story

Clare Marchant

authorHOUSE®

AuthorHouse™ UK
1663 Liberty Drive
Bloomington, IN 47403 USA
www.authorhouse.co.uk
Phone: UK TFN: 0800 0148641 (Toll Free inside the UK)
  UK Local: (02) 0369 56322 (+44 20 3695 6322 from outside the UK)

© 2023 Clare Marchant. All rights reserved.

No part of this book may be reproduced, stored in a retrieval system, or transmitted by any means without the written permission of the author.

Published by AuthorHouse 09/11/2023

ISBN: 979-8-8230-8226-6 (sc)
ISBN: 979-8-8230-8225-9 (e)

Print information available on the last page.

Any people depicted in stock imagery provided by Getty Images are models, and such images are being used for illustrative purposes only.
Certain stock imagery © Getty Images.

This book is printed on acid-free paper.

Because of the dynamic nature of the Internet, any web addresses or links contained in this book may have changed since publication and may no longer be valid. The views expressed in this work are solely those of the author and do not necessarily reflect the views of the publisher, and the publisher hereby disclaims any responsibility for them.

Foreword

When Clare was growing up and going through the terrible teen years, I remember her playing David Bowie and Kate Bush constantly in her bedroom. Back when she'd first started secondary school, it had been ABBA.
I ran the family business and played tennis at weekends, so I was a bit of an 'absent' dad, I'm afraid to say.

Clare got into a lot of trouble in her teen years, but we have resolved our differences. I'm now very proud of how she turned her life around and started her own businesses.

I wish her lots of luck with this book.

—Clare's Dad

Preface

I have decided to write my story in the hope that it might help someone else who's been struggling to get help with depression, anxiety, bipolar disorder, or addiction.
It was a difficult decision to make, as I live in a relatively small town and know it won't take long for the word to get around! Also, I have two businesses, and I really don't want them to suffer, as we've just gone through the Covid-19 years, which have been really tough on my businesses along with many others. We've managed to keep going so far, so that's a bonus.

So, here we go. Let's find out all about addiction, OCD, and being diagnosed with bipolar disorder at nearly 60 years old!

1

In September 2022, I finally got diagnosed with bipolar disorder after experiencing a massive hypomanic episode which resulted in the crisis team being called out to my home. They wanted to admit me to the unit (psychiatric ward), but I refused to go, as I'd been in it before with postnatal depression over twenty-seven years before. The crisis team couldn't find a bed, so it was agreed that I'd have home treatment, which meant a visit from the team every day. I must admit, I've never had another episode as bad as that one. What triggered it was a work event where I found myself completely out of my comfort zone. The adrenaline rushed in and helped me throughout the day. I was wired up and hadn't slept for several days leading up to the event. I'd had a phone call completely out of the blue from a producer of a reality show who wanted me to go on set and do some of the girls' nails. I took a team with me, and we just weren't prepared for how TV shows do their filming. We first had to go through security. Then we were Covid-19 tested. After that, we went to meet the producer, who told us we weren't allowed to go through to the cast members with our phones. We hadn't been told about this beforehand. I was on meds, and I needed my phone for the reminders I'd set telling me to take them. I'd also promised two clients that

I'd ring them at lunchtime. I asked if I could keep my phone, but he said no, so I arranged for him to have my phone but give it back to me during the lunch break. I understand why we couldn't have them. We could have taken photos of the cast and the venue and leaked them, I guess. The show wasn't due to be aired until April 2023. We also hadn't been told what the reality show was about, so when the cast told us, we were all a little shocked and not prepared for it at all.

We worked flat out, not stopping to have regular breaks. They did provide lunch, but although I got the girls to stop and eat, I didn't stop myself. Two of my team members were pregnant, so they needed regular breaks. I did manage to grab some water and get a loo break, but otherwise, I didn't stop all day. We were all exhausted by the demands of the cast, who already had products on their nails which were really difficult to remove. We hadn't been expecting that. They also wanted certain types of nails, which we hadn't been told about beforehand, so it was a very long and stressful day. I'd been upfront when we'd arrived and had said I thought I was on a bipolar high. I'd asked them to excuse me if I was loud and excitable and said that I'd need my meds at lunchtime. I told them everyone on my team was aware of my condition, and they would keep an eye on me. The on-site security guard had nicknames for us all—one of us was 'Makeup Girl', another was 'Pregnant Girl', and I was labelled 'Mad as a Box of Frogs'!

We left after a long day, and I then had to go to the salon to do two more clients before unloading all the products and equipment that we'd had to take with us for the filming day. We were all shattered. I sent the girls home and did the unloading myself, after which I did my other clients, who I'd arranged to come to the salon after the filming had finished. I was absolutely exhausted and hungry by the time I finally arrived home that evening.

I think now that was what made that manic episode into the worst I've ever had. I got higher and higher and started to be argumentative, and my family got really concerned, as they'd not seen me like that before. They made a decision to call the doctor, who suggested ringing the crisis team.

Since then, I've been trying to work out what triggers the manic phase and keeping a diary of mood changes, which is something I would suggest that anyone struggling with their mental health do. Keep a mood diary. One trigger for me is when things around me start going really well. It seems I then get the adrenaline flowing in a good way, not like in fight-or-flight mode. My low phases, meanwhile, are triggered when I do not feel I have control of a situation. For example, if we have a week at work where we have fewer clients, it starts me dwelling on and overthinking the situation and then getting depressed and worried with the anxiety of running a small business. Then, I can't leave the house or drive anywhere on my own. I'm scared of everything and won't go shopping. I literally just stay in bed, sleeping for up to fourteen hours at a time. I'll go to work (as not going isn't an option) and get into bed as soon as I arrive home. I get overanxious and worry about every little thing. The anxiety is crippling, and no one understands unless they have experienced it themselves.

In a manic phase I work fast and can't sleep. I fixate on what I'm doing, and my mood changes to a complete high about everything. My brain becomes overactive, and then I can't stop. That's when I'm at my most creative, and I absolutely thrive on it. But it doesn't last. When my brain becomes too overworked, it becomes dangerous. I become a risk-taker and overspend. I think everything is wonderful and that I am invincible and can do anything. I have no anxiety or worries. Without medication, my condition would escalate quickly to full on psychosis, and that's not good for me or those around me. I've found now that my medication needs to be continually tweaked by my psychiatrist.

So, during my September episode, I'd been up for days, not able to switch off my brain, working, planning, being creative, cleaning, washing, rushing around, driving fast, and spending money on things for me and the salon. Worst of all, I had no fear about anything. However, this time was different than my other episodes. I found I was laughing hysterically one minute and then crying the next. I started to get argumentative and started accusing people of hiding things from me and thinking they were all against me. I'd not had this happen before. I also kept forgetting where I put my phone and was convinced that they were hiding it, and I started to get really stressed. My daughter rang the crisis team for help. I have very little memory of the weeks that followed; it's like I blocked it all out. Apparently, it's very common to have no recollection of times like these, as the mind works overtime and then can't remember because everything happened too fast.

The crisis team arrived to assess me, and I was pacing back and forth, not able to concentrate on anything, including what they were saying. I just kept searching for my phone and was convinced they were hiding it from me. My daughters were called, and they came round to see if they could help. The team went off to find me a bed on the ward, but they were full to capacity, so I couldn't go into hospital. They recommended home care from the crisis team, as long as someone could be with me looking after me. My husband got that job, but he was due to go into hospital in Worcester for a procedure, because a few weeks before, he'd had a heart attack. Great timing! My dad had the job of staying the night and watching out for me, bless him.

That episode was the worst I'd had so far, and I don't want to have that happen again, ever. Now that I know the warning signs of going manic after the beginnings of a high, I think I can 'nip it in the bud', as they say, but I've yet to have another manic episode to see if the meds I'm now on stabilise me. I can't thank the crisis team enough. They visited me every day for two weeks during my episode and then weekly until I started to feel better. Six months later, I'm still under the care of the neighbourhood team, now with biweekly visits.

During the first few weeks of the manic episode, I had several friends visit me, but I have very little recollection of who came or what we talked about.

One word of advice I would give is not to ask other people with bipolar disorder what meds they are on. There are so many different meds, and every person is different, so talk to your psychiatrist and ask them to explain fully what each drug actually does for you.

I decided recently, after my manic episode subsequent four months of deep depression, to tell my story. I'm doing this with the objective of helping others to reach out for help before they get to the state I got to and to learn the triggers and signs of an oncoming manic episode. If I can help even just one person by writing this, then it will have been worth it.

I'm fully aware that after writing this, I may well be judged, and it's going to leave me wide open to people's opinions and views of me. However, it may help someone struggling with their mental health or addiction, so here I am, writing about my long struggle towards finally getting diagnosed with bipolar disorder.

I manage two businesses, and because I'm self-employed I can't take time off. If I did, the business wouldn't make enough money to pay the rent or the staff. That's been really hard, as if I had been employed by someone else, I would have been signed off until I stabilised. I took just two weeks off and then rushed back to work, feeling extremely anxious and still not well. I know that my friends and family may think I'm crazy for writing my life story. (I have left quite a bit out, as I don't want to upset my family.) They also think writing this will affect my business. I personally don't think it will, and if it does, then so be it. My salons were set up with the idea that they would be safe havens for those who normally wouldn't go to a hair/beauty salon because of their own fears of anxiety. I also advertise that we offer quiet appointments and even one-on-one appointments for those with really bad mental health. For those, we close the door to the salon and just have the one client in. We give them a safe, nonjudgmental place to come for their treatments. We also have wheelchair access, which is great for both wheelchair users and mums with pushchairs.

I've been looking back over my life with a different perspective, now I've been diagnosed, and it's been an eye-opener for me. I see that the signs were there all along. It's taken me until age 59 to find out what has been wrong with me and why I've done the things I've done. I've always suffered with down times and have quite often been a risk-taker at other times. I've had a very vivid imagination too. I'm going to go right back to my earliest memories for you, and maybe you can find something there that could help you along the way. I've always used journals, and I have one specific one I started in 2005. Below are a few excerpts to give you a feel for what it's like when you suffer with depression and anxiety and self-medicate to help block the feelings out.

Journal Entries

Letters to God, 2005

Lord, please help me to stop drinking. Help me to look over the events of the day and count my blessings, instead of self-medicating and feeling anxious and down.

Help me to feel I am worth something. I went to counselling today, and the female counsellor told me that I have a great sense of humour and that I am gorgeous, sexy, and fun! Help me to remember those words when I am so low. She suggested I write a Post-it note saying, 'I am gorgeous,' and stick it on the mirror, because I look in the mirror and don't like myself. Apparently, if you keep doing this, it helps. Well, I don't see what she sees! I hate what I look like and don't like being me. I understand that depression makes you see the worst. People tell you to snap out of it, but it's like being down a deep, dark pit and being unable to climb out.

I remember when I used to hurt myself when I was really depressed. I still have a big scar on the top of my leg, which I gave myself the day my grandad passed away. What a reminder! I don't think I'll forget that date—05/05/2005. I've made a conscious decision not to self-harm again, as it's ruined my arms and now my leg too.

March 2006

In my relationships, men have always ended up putting me down. They've tried to make me dependent on them and then let me down. I've realised that after having had a year on my own with no men, I feel stronger, and I can make my own choices. Why, then, do I let men take over and let myself become submissive. I am a strong person, but I allow them to control me. Why do I let this happen? Why don't I stand up for myself? I'm usually very assertive but not when it comes to relationships.

July 2006

I've decided to stop having alcohol. I haven't had a drink, and I'm trying to fill my time with other things so I don't drink. The cravings are terrible. Are they mental cravings or physical? I guess you get both when you stop suddenly.

October 2006

What's wrong with me? Why do I always try so hard to please everyone and get so upset when I can't? I just want everyone to be happy, and it's not possible. Why do I care so much what people think of me? I've come off my antidepressants yet again, and now I feel flat and irritable and have no appetite at all. When I swallow food, it feels like cardboard. I feel like I've disappeared through grief, disappointment, and anger and like the happy me isn't here anymore. I remember the counsellor saying that depression is anger turned inward. But why am I so angry? I feel like running away, packing my bags and leaving everything behind. I wonder how many people feel like I do. I know I'm supposed to pray and turn to God, but I haven't the energy or motivation.

The Early Memories

At age 4, I hid in the hedge at the bottom of the garden, not wanting to be found. I used to have vivid nightmares even at that age. They were always the same, about wolves eating me up. I guess I'd had 'Little Red Riding Hood' read to me or something!

A few years later, after moving to a bigger house, I did it again. I packed a bag and hid in the shed, taking some bread and cheese with me to keep me going. I was there ages, wondering when they would come looking for me! I guess I wanted to be found and secretly wanted to be missed and hugged and loved.

I had the same curtains that I had been so scared of in the previous house. They were red with black shapes on them, and at night, I would be too scared to look at them, because the black shapes became wolves. I also had a real fireplace in my bedroom, and I was convinced that wolves would come down the chimney and gobble me up! Consequently, my parents boarded up the fireplace. I also thought there were wolves hiding under my bed, so I'd stand by the entrance to my bedroom and leap onto the bed quickly before checking underneath. I remember sitting outside my parents' bedroom and crying, not wanting to be alone in that bedroom. My nightmares were awful most nights.

I was a lonely child, although very popular. I thought I was someone else and imagined that I was in the wrong family and that someone had taken me there and left me. I thought I really had been found under a gooseberry bush, as my dad used to joke! I felt like an imposter, someone living in the wrong house with the wrong family. I remember reading a lot—*Heidi*, *The Little Princess*, *Little House on the Prairie*. I used to pretend I was Heidi and take bread and cheese to bed with me. Or I'd pretend I was the little servant girl up in the attic in *The Little Princess* or one of the girls in *Little House on the Prairie*, who had one candy cane at Christmas and wore home-made dresses. I dressed up and wore my grandma's moccasins, which were actually real ones made for her mum by the Blackfoot tribe in Canada, where she was born right next to a First Nations reservation. Her parents had moved to Canada not knowing where they were going to be sent. They had chosen to emigrate for a new life and had travelled by ship. On arrival, they'd just been given a grid reference of where they had to live. They'd been given a plot of land on the grid reference where they travelled, and they'd built their home as a small holding. My great-grandad worked on the railway that was being built across Canada. The small holding they built was near South Qu'Appelle in Saskatchewan. My great-gran loved telling me stories of their lives, and I loved my make-believe world. I loved escaping to my fantasy world and spent hours reading books and fantasizing that I was in the story.

Living with Bipolar

My gran in Canada.

I had really severe asthma. In fact, a photo of me and some other children in hospital was featured in the local paper (Fig. 3). I spent my first Christmas in hospital in the children's ward. I didn't get any better, so I had allergy testing, which showed I was allergic to dogs, cats, and anything else that was furry, as well as house dust and grasses. My mum said that she was told that I pushed people away from me in primary school, and I think, looking back, that having asthma is why I'm claustrophobic; I need space around me to feel I can breathe. Even now, I can't cope with crowds, and my husband does our food shopping, because I hate the busy supermarkets. I don't like lifts either. Of course, this only applies when I'm in a depressive mood, not when I'm on a high.

I dreamed of becoming a famous ballerina and leaving home to join the Royal Ballet. The truth of the matter was that I was good at ballet, but when I got to secondary school, I had the mick taken out of my ballet lessons and so started skipping them. I would get dropped off at the class, run in, change clothes, and go off to the pub with my friend, aged 14.

It was a rough type of pub. I had to drink blackcurrant because I was underage, but the guys usually got me a snakebite, which I would drink when the barman wasn't looking. Eventually, my ballet teacher asked my mum why I went to ballet on weekdays but never came to the Saturday classes. My mum then found out that my best friend and I were skipping Saturdays.

Consequently, I was told that I was a bad influence on my friend, and her parents didn't want me mixing with her anymore. However, we didn't listen and are still friends until this day!

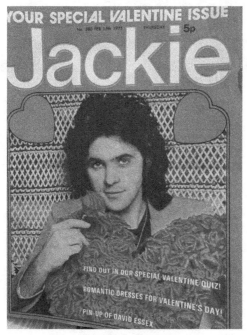

David Essex on the front cover of a 1975 edition of *Jackie* magazine.

Teen Life

I went to a Roman Catholic secondary school. My parents sent me there even though we weren't Catholic. It was smaller than the school in my catchment area, and they thought it would be better for me, being asthmatic. I had to go to Mass, which was really alien to me. I'd never experienced a Catholic service before and felt really out of my comfort zone. However, I was intrigued by the Mass, the priests drinking out of the goblet, and the nuns, who wore black and had no hair showing. My first class at school was taught by a form tutor who was called Sister Damian. She had a lot of facial hair, so I wondered if she was actually a man! Silly thoughts we have at age 11, aren't they?

As I got older, I started skipping school and lying on the Castle Green, drinking cider with older people. That was the beginning of a slippery slope into drugs and drink. I started to self-harm with razor blades and struggled with depression and severe anxiety. One day, I sat on my windowsill with a flower, picking the petals one by one and saying, 'Jump; don't jump,' until I got to the last petal. I met a boy in the year above me at school who introduced me to weed and magic mushrooms. One day, I arrived home on my bike after being at his house drinking mushroom tea, and I started staring at my mum. Her head wasn't on her body. In fact, it floated off. That's what the hallucinations did to me! How I got home that day, I don't know. I'd had to get off my bike and push it, because I'd been hallucinating going up the hill to my house. I'd thought the trees were closing in on me. When I was inside my house, I lay on the bed and experienced the worst hallucinations ever until I eventually came down off the magic mushrooms.

I met older boys in the pub and started taking different drugs just for the kick. I didn't care what they were, either; I just accepted the pills I was given and swallowed them, not caring what they did. It was fun. I felt exhilarated and briefly happy. I wanted excitement, danger, and thrills and took risks. I dyed my hair black and started wearing hippy-type clothes. I hated who I was and hated what I looked like, and my self-esteem was zero. I looked for love in all the wrong places. I saw and experienced things a young girl of 14 should never have seen or experienced. I hung around with an older guy who was an alcoholic. I even took him home with me, and my mum said, 'Oh, I thought you'd brought him home for me!' joking about the age difference. I then had a boyfriend who was a heroin addict. Looking back, I can't believe that as a young teenager, I mixed with people who were addicts. He later died. I got to know how to divide speed up and how to sniff it up my nose through a rolled-up note. I got searched by the police several times, but luckily for me, I didn't have any drugs on me. The worst that happened was that I got caught shoplifting. It was so embarrassing, having the police called to the local Boots store, especially as it was only an eye pencil! It was just a dare someone had given me. I was given a caution, and my lovely gran, who I was really close to, came to fetch me.

There was a club called the Rotters' Club where they had live bands, and a couple of friends and I would go there and meet our art teacher, who was always friendly to us. The bands were great, and we obviously drank underage.

The next episode was going off on motorbikes round the forest areas with the Hell's Angels and hanging out at various pubs. By then, I was 16 years old. I had moved on from junkies to bikers. I wanted a ride. I wanted to feel the speed of the bike and feel the elements around me. I loved going as fast as possible on the bikes. I soon became 'property of —' and proudly wore a denim jacket with that written on the back. Their parties were wild and usually involved fighting, drink, drugs, and occasionally a shotgun or two! I left school, left home, moved into a bedsit with my biker boyfriend, and got a job. Believe it or not, the job was as a make-up consultant in a chemist. Who was to know that years later, I would go to college to do beauty therapy.

During this time, I witnessed a terrible bike accident. Lots of us were out on the bikes, going round a bend, and one biker lost control. The bike crashed, and we obviously went flying past the crash on the bikes.

We turned around and went back to the spot where we had passed them and saw them lying on the ground. The guy looked bad, with blood all over him. The girl looked OK, so we assumed she was. Big mistake. The bikers flagged down a passing car and put her in the car with me. I sat there with my arm around her, hearing her breath making a whistling sound. The bikers went off to her house to wait for us. They didn't call an ambulance at the scene of the crash. We arrived at her house, and the guys carried her in and placed her on the sofa. I sat next to her and realised she'd wet herself, which wasn't a good sign. The ambulance arrived then, but it was too late. She was just 18 years old, and it was her birthday. I said, 'Goodbye. Who were you "property of"?'

There were a lot of things the bikers did, and I was usually there when they had their parties and get-togethers. I thought nothing of the fighting that went on, as I was usually drinking, so it didn't bother me. There were quite a few times when things got really out of hand. We'd have lock-ins regularly and drink all night. One night, we took over a pub and watched *The Texas Chainsaw Massacre* and *The Driller Killer* while high on drink and drugs. I've never been able to bring myself to watch those since.

Anyone who wanted to become a member had to prove themselves to the bikers and go through initiation. I never saw the initiations, but I believe they had to do some horrific things. These were usually done in the forest area not too far away from the town I lived in.

I didn't care much about what was going on. I was just 'property of —', so I wasn't expected to have an opinion. We just hung out in groups and went for fast rides around the area.

Becoming a Mum

I started another chapter in my life. I got pregnant and then got married—the wrong way round to do it! I was 18 years old, 19 when my beautiful baby girl was born. She was something so amazing and precious amid a life full of danger and troubles. I held her in my arms and vowed I'd love her forever and would give her everything I had. I vowed I'd make us a good life, a clean life, with no more drink or drugs, no risk-taking, no danger, and no thrills. I sadly left my husband just before she was born, worried about the lifestyle we had been leading.

One night, the president of the bikers chapter turned up at my flat. I didn't want to let him in, as I wasn't sure what he'd come for. He walked past me and asked where my baby was. I felt I had no option but to show him. He bent over the cot and touched her face. I was petrified. I thought he was going to take her, but instead, he reached into his pocket and took out some money, which he put under the pillow for her. Then it was just me and my baby.

Looking back now, I can see the periods of deep depression when I used to self-harm to feel something. I can see the ups, the highs, when I took risks and didn't care what I did. I had been diagnosed with OCD and had CBT to try to help. Everyone thought I was just troubled, but I think now that it was possibly the beginnings of bipolar disorder. Maybe I've always had it. It certainly would explain the lows and highs I always suffered from.

New Beginnings

When my baby girl was 6 months old, I enrolled in college and did my BTEC in finance. I also worked nights in a pub to be able to make ends meet. Obviously, my days were spent with my daughter. After I successfully completed my BTEC, I got a job working for a computer company. I hoped I'd be able to get a mortgage and buy a flat for us to live in instead of the council flat where we were currently residing. I still partied at weekends and drank quite a lot. No drugs, though! I still suffered with bouts of depression and was put on antidepressants.

I saved up and went on holiday to Ibiza with a friend of mine, leaving my daughter with my mum. We partied hard at night and slept on the beach in the day. We went clubbing, and I met a guy who was Swiss. Then came the classic holiday romance. He hired a scooter, and we went around the island, carefree and having fun. When it was time for me to leave, we swapped addresses, and he said he'd fly over and come visit me, which he did a couple of weeks later. The next thing you know, I was packing up, leaving my flat, and moving to Switzerland with my daughter to be with him. I believed I was in love. It lasted three weeks until I came down to earth, went through a depressive stage, and left him. I came back to England and my flat, which I'd rented out, and started looking for a job. He died in a motorbike accident a few weeks after I came home. I've still got a necklace he gave to me which says, 'Ich Liebe Dich' ('I love you').

I applied for a job in a building society. It was a temporary job, but they offered me a full-time role. I trained as a mortgage adviser and met someone I fell in love with. We bought a house together and had a child together a couple of years later. Unfortunately, I got postpartum psychosis, which is a form of postnatal depression. Things weren't good, and I got hospitalised and after a few weeks. (The baby was in hospital with me.) I didn't want to come home. I felt safe and well looked after in hospital and made friends with lots of the patients. I ended up quite liking it in the hospital psychiatric ward. I didn't want to leave the safety of the ward.

It was a crazy place to be with a baby, but there were no mother-and-baby units in those days. My dad came to visit me, and a girl literally ran into the communal room and started stripping off her clothes. Dad found that quite funny, but I think he was quite shocked I was there in the ward with this type of situation happening around me.

I made friends with others who were there, and it became my safe haven. I got day release to go home, and when I got there, I couldn't get out of the car. So, I went back to the ward for a bit longer. I just wanted to be looked after and not have the outside stressors. I remember seeing my eldest child waiting on the doorstep for me, and I couldn't even get out of the car.

I then trained as a financial advisor and got a new job. I worked with all guys, and they drank a lot. I tried to keep up with them and blacked out frequently after the binge drinking. One time, I was in a car being taken home after a big binge, and I decided to open the car door and try to jump out! When I drank, I became the life and soul of the party, but I could never have just one drink. Just one led to more and more until I either became silly and flirtatious or depressed and sad. Drink changes you. It can make any inhibitions go out the window, or it can make you depressed. I think it depends on the mood you are in already when drinking. One thing was for sure: I couldn't have just one drink and stop.

About six months after being in hospital with postpartum psychosis, I was incredibly low and was walking along the high street. I saw a church and felt drawn to go inside. There was a service on, and I felt really awkward pushing a pram inside. However, the place seemed very welcoming. I listened intently to the sermon. I felt God was talking directly to me! The pastor was talking about the fact that if we felt we had done things wrong in our lives, we each needed to imagine putting all the bad things in a black bin bag, carrying that bag on our shoulders, and then dumping it at the foot of the cross and asking Jesus to forgive our sins. It really made an impact on me, so I stayed behind after the service to ask more about it. I then joined an alpha course to learn and explore more about becoming a Christian. I consequently made a decision to become a Christian and started going to church every Sunday.

I still struggled with the depression, and unfortunately, my partner and I split up after five years. I must have been really hard to live with, being depressed all the time. It was hard on us all, especially as he worked away for long periods and left me on my own with two children.

The Next Chapter

A couple of years later, I met someone through work. He'd come to fix the computers. Within a few days, I was 'in love', and we got married after a few months and had another baby. That didn't end well. He ended up going to prison for seven years due to armed robbery. I was left with three children and bills to pay. So, I carried on working, bought a house, and moved area. He'd run up debts, but because I was a financial adviser, I knew how to contact the bank and work out a repayment plan. It gave me my first taste of negotiating how to pay back debts. I then started helping my friend, who had been diagnosed with cancer, with her debts and teaching her how to negotiate with the various companies. In doing so, I realised I wanted to help other people get out of debt. I felt that because I'd gone through arranging payments with my creditors, I could now help others who hadn't the benefit of a financial background. My husband got out of prison four years later, and I let him back into my life. After two weeks, I realised I'd not had my usual credit card statement, so while at work, I rang the bank. I was shocked to hear there was a balance of £3,000 on my account. I'd given him a second chance and put his name on my account so he could have a card too. He'd told me he was going to open a business and only put £500 on the card. I then did a search on my name to get my credit file. There I found another two cards in my name which I hadn't opened. He had applied in my name and then waylaid the postman to get my post and subsequently the cards. I went home devastated and had no choice but to report him to the parole board and also the police. I was going to have to pay back the one card, as I'd willingly put his name as an additional account holder, but the others, luckily, were written off as fraudulent. He had to go back to prison to finish his time there.

I started working for a Christian charity that helped people who were in debt. I was still drinking in the evenings. It seemed to be the one thing I couldn't give up. I tried to hide it from Christian friends and thought I was living a bit of a lie, but I had a faith in God and went to church every Sunday. I worked hard, though, and it didn't affect my ability to do my job. I did this part time, along with being a financial adviser, until I left my financial adviser job and started running the debt centre from our church. I loved going out to see families that were in debt and being able to take the weight off their minds while I negotiated with the creditors for them. I saw all sorts of families from all different backgrounds. I volunteered to do pamper sessions at the church for some of the families I met so that they could have something lovely to look forward to. Most had never experienced a facial or a pedicure, so it was a real treat for them. I really loved doing those sessions and seeing people enjoy them. I ran the debt centre and managed a team of volunteers there for nearly ten years and carried on going to church. That was the most stable time of my life, because everything I did I was doing for God and because I had church family to turn to if I started to go into a depression. To some degree, it helped me stop going out partying, and I did cut down how much I was drinking.

Journal Entries

August 2007

I've made a vow to God that I won't look for a partner and that I will dedicate my life to serving Him. I won't have a relationship with a non-Christian and will wait however long it takes to find a Christian partner. I prayed for a new job too. This came when one of the church leaders asked if I wanted to help people in debt. I've been a financial adviser, and I helped my friend when her electric and gas had been cut off. I even went with her as her advocate when the building society applied to evict her and her five children from their home, and we managed to put a stop to it. So, I've started a new chapter in my life of working for the church, going out and seeing families in debt and helping them budget.

October 2007

Well, what a year 2007 has been. I had painful months of recovering from being betrayed by someone close to me. My pastor and his wife moved to Newcastle. One of my good friends moved to France. My very good friend was diagnosed with a brain tumour in April. I spent time with her when she couldn't talk properly. I took her for her first session of chemotherapy. Another time, we drove with the window open, and her hair was flying out through the open window. I went to visit her when she was in the hospice, and she couldn't speak at all then. She died in July. I was devastated, as I'd spent my time with her and missed her so much.

Marrying a Pastor

After five years of living on my own with the children, I met someone. He was a pastor of a church. We met in July and were married by December! While still managing the debt centre, I went to college two nights a week; my husband had the children those nights. I did a Level 2 in beauty therapy and then spent another year doing Level 3. Then I did my teaching qualification and set up a training academy. Meanwhile, I was still drinking and still having really bad periods of depression. I tried many, many times to quit alcohol.

I went for a psychiatric evaluation, but they wouldn't diagnose me, due to me still drinking. My husband stood by my side. He'd even had to carry me out of a function before because I'd passed out. My brother's wedding was one of the worst incidents—not because of the wedding itself but because of my binge. I passed out on a sofa, so my husband sat with me for a couple of hours, telling people I was ill and just sleeping. In reality, I'd passed out. Some may ask, why did he put up with it? He never judged me for drinking and never told me not to drink. He said if he told me not to, I'd do the opposite, so he just made sure I was safe.

There were many times when we went out together and I ended up having too much to drink. He didn't drink, so he'd drive us home. I used to be unable to get out of the car and would sit there counting from one to ten over and over until my anxiety had passed and I was able to go inside the house. One time, I took an hour just to be able to get into the house. What I didn't realise was that the next day, I'd be extra anxious, and I believe that is what happens when you drink too much. Well, it's certainly what happened for me!

Once, we went to visit his birth mother, and I remember sitting down to have dinner. The wine was poured, and I finished mine really quickly. I thought it wasn't polite to ask for more, so I had to wait until the glasses were all refilled, which wasn't quick enough for me. His mum gave us a bag full of alcohol to take home for our wedding, and then everyone else went to bed. What I did was find the bag and start on the vodka. The next morning, his mum got the bag out, and I was so embarrassed when she saw the vodka she'd put in it was now half empty!

We took it all home and put it on top of the kitchen cupboard. Bad idea. I helped myself most nights until every bottle was empty. I put them back, so it looked like they were still full. My husband got one down to have a drink, saying he just wanted to try the nice bottle of wine that was up there. He found all the empty bottles, and I was mortified. Because he doesn't usually drink, I never for one moment thought he'd get the bottles down, and I had been drinking them over a period of time.

Journal Entries

July 2012

I've met someone! He came to preach at my church. There was an immediate connection, and I went on a date. We have both had experience being in debt, getting divorced, and looking after our children. Believe it or not, I have a list of what a partner has to be like. I've found my man, and he has all the attributes on my list! I can't believe he asked me to marry him on our second date!

December 2012

I've gotten married! The wedding was like a dream, and everything went to plan. We were married by my husband's best friend in the church I met him in and where I work.

A few years after getting married, I had a massive blowout on gin and was so drunk that I even rang my son's dad and asked him to come and fetch me. (He didn't, by the way!) My daughter tipped the rest of the gin down the sink. I screamed at her and grabbed the bottle, but it was empty. I was absolutely fuming and needed more booze. I realised this had to stop, so I started going to AA.

September 2013

There is a constant battle within each of us, whether it's about drinking too much, eating too much, or exercising to excess. It's the battle between right and wrong, good and bad, the light and the darkness. Do people make you feel good or bad? Do they lift you up or put you down? Surround yourself with like-minded people who build you up, not bring you down. Choose friends that see the best. Look for the good things and reflect on the positives. Depression is real. It can be all-consuming, and you feel like you're in a deep, dark pit with no way to climb out. Life feels pointless. The use of drink, drugs or even food gives a temporary high and helps you escape from the pain. Deep hurts are temporarily masked, and for a moment, the pain goes away. For a moment, you don't feel anything. It's numbed by drink, drugs, food, or even self-harm. However, it doesn't last, and your body starts to crave more and more to get the same effect you felt before. It's a vicious circle. You can, in fact, experience a physical and mental craving, and if you don't have what you are craving, you feel anxious and stressed. The power and pull of addictions can be so overwhelming. How can we break this cycle? Admit that we are powerless and that we need God or our higher power. We can't do this on our own. Try to help others. Choose positive thoughts and push the negative ones away.

December 2013

Take responsibility for your actions. Actions speak louder than words, so choose to act and not react. Treat people the way you'd like to be treated. Think of positive things. If you fall down, get back up and keep moving forward. Don't think of the past or the future, just the present moment. Take one step at a time. Try to go out for a walk or do some exercise, as this will help. But I feel too down to even attempt to leave the house, let alone do an exercise class.

January 2014

I've bought vodka and hidden it in the cupboard. I drink tonic water, but of course, I sneak the vodka in. I think everyone thinks I'm just drinking tonic. I've hidden the vodka. I sneak out and refill my glass and think no one knows, but they probably do. Drink numbs the pain. It helps me escape and enables me to be reckless, to take risks, and to do what I want. I can't give it up. I've tried, and it's torture! Sometimes I last a week, sometimes six months, but you can guarantee that a crisis will happen and I'll pick up again. God, I hate myself. Why am I so weak?

October 2014

Well, what a couple of days. I decided to give up alcohol. The insomnia is the worst. I can't sleep. I keep thinking of having a drink, but there is none in the house. I had an operation on my knee and got a chest infection to top it off. I couldn't smoke or drink alcohol, so what an ideal time to give them up. I'm thinking of how I usually get home from work and drink a lovely bottle of champagne, prosecco, or cava. I fantasise about opening the first bottle, hearing the pop of the cork, pouring that first drink, and watching the bubbles before taking my first sip. I fantasise about that taste and the relief that comes after. I hold the first sip in my mouth and swish it around, just loving that taste and the instant buzz that comes from that first drink. The trouble is, one turns into more and more each time. I give in after a couple of weeks and go out and buy vodka. I hide it in the cupboard and sneak some into my glass of tonic water, thinking no one has noticed. I'm hiding it wherever I can. I'm deceiving the people I love, but I can't stop. It's got its hold on me again.

I decided after another failed attempt to give up alcohol to go to AA. I didn't know where the AA meetings were held, so I phoned the helpline. They told me they would get someone in my area to ring me. Later, I had a phone call from a lovely lady who put me in touch with someone I could meet for a coffee and a chat. I arranged it and went, feeling really nervous. We met, and I told her the story of my struggles. She suggested I go to a meeting with her. They were all so helpful and supportive. I attended ninety meetings in ninety days. I had quit! It's now been five years since I've had a drink.

The trick is to imagine one drink. You know it will lead to more and end in a blackout. You know you're going to send crazy text messages, which you'll regret the next morning. You play the scenario forward in your head before you pick up a drink. When you want a drink, think what will happen and imagine yourself hung-over the next day, having made some huge mistakes the night before. This will help you not to pick up that first drink, which will always lead to more. AA has been my lifeline, along with my faith.

I've made lots of friends through AA. To anyone who realises they drink too much, wants to stop, but can't, I suggest that they go to AA. It really helps having other people around from all backgrounds with whom you can share your story. We all have similar traits, and we all understand each other. It really is a lifeline. The meetings are all confidential. What is said in the rooms stays in the rooms.

They even say the serenity prayer at the end, and all hold hands while saying it: 'God, give me the grace to accept the things that cannot be changed, the courage to change the things that can be changed, and the wisdom to know the difference.'

February 2018

Well, I can't do it, so I need help. I decided to go to AA. I found people that were like me from all walks of life. I listen to their stories and realised I'm not alone. I've gone to ninety meetings in ninety days. I learned that once you have a sip and pick up that first drink, you'll want more and more. So, I'm just taking it one day at a time. I am happy to say that I've now been alcohol free for just over five years!

Moving Forward

Life is good. I've been married ten years; I have three children, four step-children, and seven grandchildren; I have two businesses and employ staff; and I don't drink. However, I still have periods of depression and periods of feeling really 'up'. Sometimes, it's crippling, and Covid hasn't helped. I got used to not going out of the house, so it was a shock going back to work and suddenly facing people again. My anxiety was sky high. The depression set in again. I really struggled, because I'd gotten used to being at home and in my safe environment. I didn't have to go out and face people. However, I found running a business extremely stressful.

Last year in May, I woke up one day feeling excited and talking fast. I rushed around cleaning the house, going out driving, going shopping, and impulse buying, and I got no sleep at all for nearly two weeks. I made huge plans for the business. I spent money buying courses for the girls and equipment for the salon, so I decided to go see a GP. I thought it might be bipolar disorder, as I'd started to read up on it, but I wasn't sure. The GP took me off my antidepressants and told me to see how that went. I slipped back into a deep depression and went back to the GP, who put me back on antidepressants!

I'd started a refresher hairdressing course, and the first week I went, I had no confidence. I felt extremely anxious and worried about how I'd perform. In the weeks before it began, I even worried about driving there, where I would park, and so on. So, I'd gone there the week before to suss out the parking. A week after starting the course, I woke up manic. There was no reason for it at all, just a complete change in mood. This seemed to settle until the course finished in July, at which point I slipped back into a deep depression. I was sleeping fourteen hours a night (going to bed at 5 p.m.) and feeling anxious. I avoided shopping, cleaning, and going out anywhere. Working and running a business was really hard during this time.

Then, in September, I went into another manic phase, rushing around, speaking fast, overspending, coming up with massive ideas for the business, not sleeping at all, being up all night planning, and overthinking everything. I look back now at September and October, and I have no memory of what I did, no memory of friends who visited or people I saw. That's really scary. It takes me back to the blackouts I'd have after a drinking session.

Fast forward to now. I'm back at work and still under the care of the neighbourhood team. Thank goodness for that, because this week, I haven't slept since Tuesday. It's now Friday evening, and I'm feeling all those feelings again. But because I now know the signs, I've been able to ring the mental health team and tell them what's going on. Hopefully this time, it won't go to mania but will settle back down with the pills I have been prescribed. It's always a case of tweaking the medication, because everyone is different and what works for one person doesn't necessarily work for another.

I know the warning signs now, and I've joined Bipolar UK, where they have peer support. I'm hoping that I can keep this under control now. I will have it for the rest of my life, they have told me, and I need to keep the stresses and triggers under control. My husband is really supportive and knows the signs now, so he can point out to me if I'm going into a depression or going into a manic episode. He's stood by my side through the drinking and the bipolar. He does the shopping, cooks our meals, and even drives me to work if I'm anxious. He does all this whilst running a church, with all that that entails.

I hope that this book may be of some help to you if you have experienced any of these episodes and that you will be able to go and ask for help. Don't keep it to yourself; tell someone. Ring someone and get help. The crisis team have supported me since September, when I had the worst manic episode I've ever had. The support is still ongoing, only it's decreased to one visit every two weeks from the community psychiatric nurse.

Finally, I'm going to share some thoughts from old friends of mine below.

Memories from Friends

Kim. I remember Clare. She and her boyfriend, a Hell's Angel, used to go to the same pub as me, a bikers' pub. She was (and still is) absolutely stunning. She's petite with a fabulous figure and long, wavy hair, and she is incredibly pretty. The rest of us girls were a bit in awe. She and her boyfriend were very much the 'it couple', her boyfriend being a very handsome man with long, dark, curly hair. We were all a bit jealous.

Wendy. Clare's always been a great friend, and over the years, we've created some fantastic memories. But I always remember her being very impulsive, often running full speed into a relationship or situation without thinking it through or considering the consequences. You couldn't reason with her. She had to do it, and she was always convinced that she was happy and that everything was different this time. Waiting wasn't an option. Looking back, I think she was quite manic at times, but she always wanted to love and be loved.

Liz. Clare and I went to the same ballet school. We became friends as we danced together. I admired her lovely skin, her beauty, and her ability to dance so well. I was excited when she invited me to stay over one weekend. We spent hours in her bedroom beautifying ourselves, reading *Jackie* magazines, and singing all the words to ABBA songs! My dad, who was a very aggressive man, stopped me seeing her. I was so upset. I didn't see her for some months, which seemed like forever.

She has always worked hard. She went into finance and then worked for the church. Now, she's got her own businesses, and we still keep in touch. I've never seen her as ill as I did last September. It was awful.

Mandy. Clare was my high school friend. She was very popular with the boys, and she knew it! I think most of the girls were jealous of that. She was clever and pretty and always achieved what she set out to do, whether at school or when we left. I admire her for getting to where she is today, because her path along the way was not always easy. We may not see each other much now, but when we do, we talk of our school days with fond memories and good times.

The Story of a Fellow Bipolar Sufferer

Chamomile (not her real name) was diagnosed with bipolar I thirty years ago. She uses self-management techniques and low levels of medication to keep a balance in her life. After having been off medication for three years, she has recently chosen to go back on medication to prevent periods of depression and anxiety.

She was a high achiever with a career in the Royal Navy. She has worked as a self-employed beauty therapist and as a lecturer in beauty therapy, and she has also worked for the NHS. Now, however, Chamomile is taking time out to be creative, and she takes one day at a time.

In her words, 'There have been periods in my life where alcohol has played a part in my attempts to manage my mood levels and anxiety. I'm presently reducing the amount of alcohol I drink by taking Naltrexone medication. Unfortunately, it is not readily available via the NHS, so I pay privately for my medication. My hope is that Naltrexone will be available via the NHS in the future to help others reduce their alcohol consumption or stop drinking alcohol completely in a safe and controlled way.'

Life Now

Since writing this book things are now different for me to some degree. I've learnt some self help techniques and I try to be aware of my mood changing. I also now know where to go for help.

I keep an online mood diary, you can find this on <u>www.bipolaruk.org</u>. This enables me to track my mood, my sleep and my medication. I used to keep a paper diary but this is so much easier to use. It even gives a graph to help you try and make sense of your moods and to try and work out if there is a pattern to the moods.

My depression seems to last four to six weeks followed by hypomania for one to two weeks. I would say that at the time of writing this I haven't managed to reach a state of balance. My meds are being reviewed and the next step is to take lithium which I don't want to have to take so I've now embarked on a better diet to try and help avoid a change of meds. I'm currently exploring the fact that gut health effects brain function.

What effects does depression have?
Sleeping Lots
Severe Anxiety
Not being able to go shopping or drive
Avoiding people and places
Fear of life and no motivation to get out of bed
Avoiding friends and family
Spending little money and worrying about money
Avoiding social media and not answering emails
Not eating at all
Being scared to meet new clients

What effects does hypomania have?
Not sleeping much at all and struggling to get to sleep
Excessive shopping and driving anywhere with no fear
Making lots of plans to meet friends
Going out all the time and not staying at home
An overwhelming feeling of euphoria
Being excited about the future
Overspending and buying things I wouldn't normally buy
Doing work emails late into the night
Scrolling social media excessively
Planning work events, promotions and special events
Looking forward to meeting new clients
How do I now manage my moods?

In a hypomanic mood I get up to date with emails and social media and work late into the night so I need to put a cap on my time. I clean the house excessively and keep laundry up to date. I meet friends that I've avoided and family so I need to make sure I can keep my commitments and not make too many plans. I read books to try and relax and get to sleep however, I can suffer with a lack of concentration. I go swimming and keep active and try and get lots of fresh air. I meditate and listen to podcasts to help me relax and get to sleep. I make sure I self care and look after myself with a massage once a month. I make sure I'm eating the right foods and food that helps the brain. Most of all I try and love myself.

I hope that this book may be of some help to you if you have experienced any of these episodes and that you will be able to go and ask for help. Don't keep it to yourself; tell someone. Ring someone and get help. The crisis team have supported me since September, when I had the worst manic episode I've ever had. The support is still ongoing, only it's now a monthly phone call with my psychiatrist.

My Madness
Becky Topham

This flamboyant soul
Is often intertwined
With euphoric excess
And crisp white wine

It loves a party
It loves to chatter
The subject negligible
It doesn't matter

Mania is fun
I feel it in my bones,
The sad thing is..
I experience it all alone

Clare Marchant

And it drives away
Those I adore
Whispers and reprimands
The slam of a door

Depression my nemesis
Is an unrelenting square
Of blackest black
A self constructed lair

It staggers beside me
A beggar of sorts
Extracting from me
All positive thoughts

Yet, I am so much more
Than bipolar disorder
Try to see me first
In this very order:

I am a mum
A wife and nurse
Loyal friend and colleague
These blessings come first
Places to get help:

Bipolar UK (email: info@bipolaruk.org)

AA (www.alcoholic-anonymous.org.uk/contact)

The website sinclairmethoduk.com.

The YouTube video entitled 'Claudia Christian on Alcohol Use Disorder, the Sinclair Method, and Women and Alcohol'.

The Facebook page of The Sinclair Method.

Printed in the USA
CPSIA information can be obtained
at www.ICGtesting.com
LVHW041248051023
760079LV00002B/692

9 798823 082266